TRAVIS
STONE

A BLURRED REALITY

ISIS, POWER, TERROR, & DECEPTION

A BLURRED REALITY
ISIS, POWER, TERROR, & DECEPTION

Made in the United States of America

2 4 6 8 10 9 7 5 3 1

Published under license by
Createspace Independent Publishing Platform
& Amazon Digital Services ltd

ISBN-10: 1503080978
ISBN-13: 978-1503080973

Table of Contents

Part One
Middle Earth: Middle Eastern Terror

Part Two
The War of Terror

Author's Note

Threads of Deception: The Rise of ISIS

The rise of ISIS appears unusual, shocking, and abrupt to us in the West. ISIS' rise however, is both inevitable and predictable to those in Washington, and anyone else up to speed with the history underlying Middle Eastern terror cells.

As it happens, I've just this minute finished a book of that very title: *The Rise of ISIS*, by Jay Sekulow, and besides a nasty taste, it leaves me deeply disturbed for several strange and frightening reasons.

Unfortunately Sekulow's, *The Rise of ISIS,* is a clear piece of propaganda; it is propaganda however, penned by an infamous American Lawyer; the foreword written no less, by Oxford scholar, Harry Hutchinson.

What Sekulow does in this very popular work is to highlight the horrific atrocities committed by ISIS (which include filmed beheadings, rape, and child murder) and then align ISIS with the Palestinian Government, Hamas.

The goal of Sekulow's book therefore, is not to inform you on the critical historical elements that caused the rise of the world's most horrific terrorist network, but to make the *Palestinian* people appear to be, not only as bad as ISIS, but aligned with them.

This premise is a falsehood designed to provide support and justification for Israel's Nazi-like treatment and blockade of Palestinians since 1948.

Jay Sekulow is, of course, Jewish.

Sekulow, like many other academics that commentate on this topic, skews the truth and warps the facts regarding the rise of the horrific terrorist mindsets possessed by Al Qaeda and their offspring, The Islamic State of Iraq & Syria (ISIS) - skewing the truth for political reasons.

Later in this work I will uncover the real issues leading to the rise of Middle Eastern Terror cells; issues which are worlds apart from the formation of Hamas, the creation of Israel, and the persecution of Palestinian Arabs, rudely in the way of the chosen people and their Promised Land.

Now that may sound anti Semitic, but I am certainly not anti Israel, nor am I anti Semitic, but the *reality* - which is blurred by media driven half-truths, propaganda, and misinformation - is that the histories of ISIS, (now IS), and Hamas are completely separate.

Hamas is certainly a danger to Israel, but they are so for reasons which may seem justified to some degree, once the reality of their history is known and understood - I personally believe in non-violence, and therefore cannot support Hamas' actions - but neither have I been driven off my land and had my home bulldozed to make way for 'the chosen ones', so I have no way of knowing my reaction; I did loose my home in an earthquake, and found that distressing enough without *human persecution* behind the destruction.

IS on the other hand, is a very different beast.

IS presents as a danger to *anyone* within its reach, especially those in the Islamic world. IS' goal appears to be to force a new, more violent version of Jihadist Islam on the peoples of the Middle East; force and wage civil war in Iraq and Syria; steal all they can; toppling any and every regime, and taking over the region by force.

With my curiosity and interest lying in Cold War history - and as Middle Eastern terrorist groups arose in the Cold War vacuum, I seek to answer the questions quivering on the tips of our tongues.

To know our reality however, always requires a change in belief, because deception underlies all we are told regarding the Middle East.

Because of what we are taught, and our generational exposure to propaganda, we unwittingly see the world through a prearranged filter of deception.

Beliefs however, even those outside of reality, are ingrained and incredibly hard to change.

Tom Engelhardt, of the *American Empire Project*, cites a strange and interesting conversation between Journalist Ron Suskind, and Karl Rove (Senior Advisor to George. W. Bush). The essence of Rove's conversation is this:

> Journalists and commoners [in] "the reality based community believe that solutions (to humanity's problems) emerge from judicious study of discernable reality." But, "That's not the way the world works anymore."
>
> Rove went on to say: "We're an Empire now, and when we act we create our own reality. And while you're studying that reality - judiciously, as you will - we'll act again, creating other, new realities, which you can study too. And that's how things will sort out. We're history's actors - and you, all of you - will be left to just study what we do."

Senior Advisors, as we will see, are the most dangerous people in U.S. policy making.

Now, I am no apologist for terrorism. I hate it. In this work I will *not* seek to justify *any* act of terrorism. However, because we are lied to regarding Western actions in the Middle East, and have been since the days of the British Empire, huge interest now revolves around big questions - questions that appear complex and 'foggy'; like: how and why has IS *really* arisen?

The issues are, in actual fact, mostly simple - the fogginess shrouding Mideast unrest comes purely from deception - Western deception - deception designed for us. But as we know, where there is deception, there is a deceiver - and where there is a deceiver, there is a secret.

So it stands that in the chapters following I will answer the following questions (and more):

What led to the re-formation of Israel?

What was Israel's solution to the 'Arab problem'?

Who were the players, and what were the side-effects of the fateful triangle linking Israel, Palestine, and The United States of America? And what are the real links between the modern Muslim world and manufactured Islamic Jihad?

How, when, and why did anti Western terrorist groups form in the Middle East?

What happened in the vacuum of the Cold War to trigger the current global terror situation?

Why did Al Qaeda really attack America on September 11, 2001?

Why has the 'War on Terror' only worsened the problem of Middle Eastern terrorism; and why has ISIS or IS arisen in such a horrific wave of violence?

Does IS have an endgame? What is their goal?

In the Middle East, what secret could possibly lead to 67 years of deception?

In answering these questions and more, I want to bring balance to a subject pregnant with military, industrial, and political deception; and a subject polarized by religious affiliations.

In the following pages, I hope to clear some of a blurred reality.

Travis Stone, 11 September 2014, Oxford

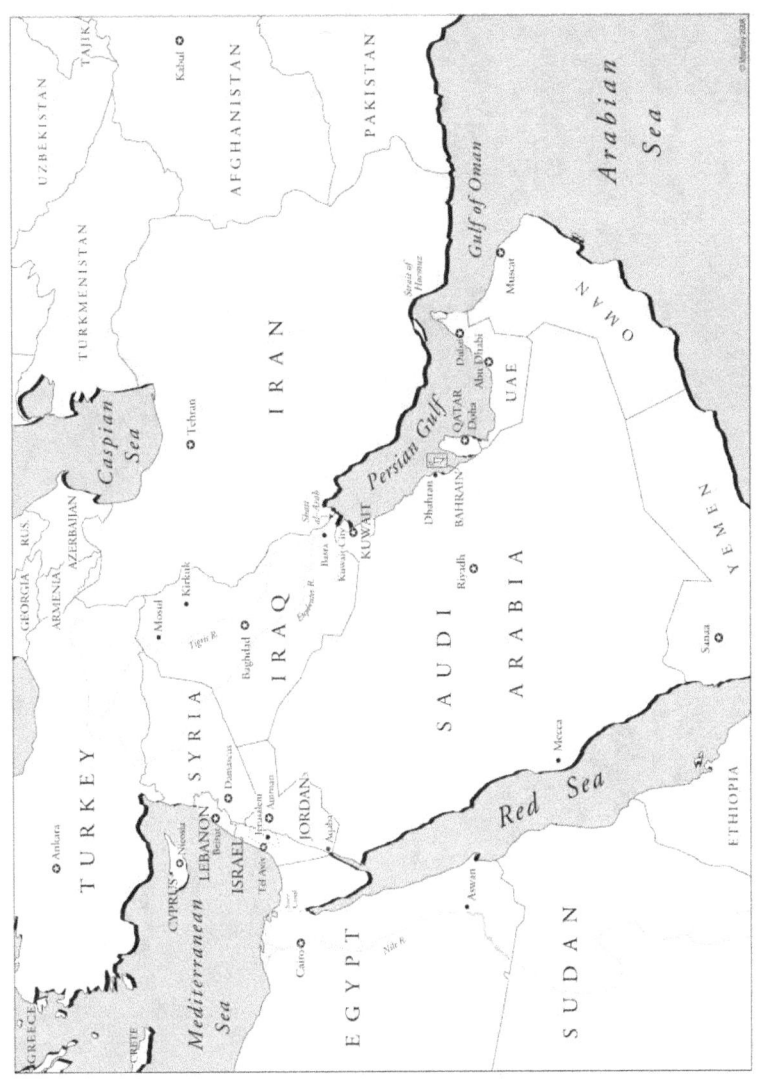

Part One

Middle Earth: Middle Eastern Terror

1

Age of Empires

To Kingdom Come

In 1914 the British ruled her Empire through the aggressive exploitation of her colonies, maintained by brutal and violent control.

Britain's goals regarding the First World War (1914-18) were twofold:

> 1) Militarily crush and remove the (Muslim) Ottoman Empire from Central Europe, and take control of their Middle Eastern oil countries, and;[1]

> 2) Seize the area of Palestine in preparation for Zionization, and the *(re)*creation of Israel, the holy-land; and the repatriation of the Zionist Jewish peoples.[2]

Of course, no one in the West at the time was greatly opposed to these outcomes, they were seen as mostly good;

---

1. Stone. A Time for Deception
2. Ibid

the Arab Palestinians however, may have foreseen their coming fate, but no one in Western world cared what Muslims thought then.

Standard Oil of America, the big oil company of the age, may never have imagined (not even in their wildest dreams) just how massively dependent on oil the world would become in the distant future, but they certainly knew the implications regarding the economic and military power in their own time.

In 1918 the French politician Henri Berenger was quoted saying: "Oil is recognized today to be as necessary as blood."[3] And: "He who controls the oil will control the world."[4]

The British Empire knew where the oil lay; they knew this because of a detailed geological survey of the world's likely oil reserves, (drillable and not-drillable) conducted by Herbert Hoover, and completed in 1920.[5] In 1929 Hoover was, of course, elected the 31st President of the United States.

Overcoming squeamishness: Kurds & Whey

The British obviously sort to dominate the oil rich Middle East so as to secure and guarantee military dominance in future wars. (Despite WWI being sold to the people as, 'The war to end all wars").

---

3. McBeth. *British Oil Policy*

4. *Ibid*

5. Marshall Douglas Smith. *Black Gold Hot Gold*

> [At] WWI's end, the massive territories of The Ottoman Empire were divided between France and Britain, with Russia carving off some of Turkey. Standard Oil representatives, Bernard Baruch, Paul Warburg, and 'Colonel' House, participated in the Treaty of Versailles negotiations, which secured Standard Oil's interests in the region.[6]

Prior to WWI, The Ottoman or Turkish Empire held today's following territories (and more): The former Yugoslavia; Turkey; Iran; Iraq; Syria; Lebanon; the current region of Israel; North Africa, including Algiers, Libya, and Egypt; and also a strip of Saudi Arabia containing Medina and Mecca.

Basically the Ottomans held the regions containing the world's largest known oil deposits and their sea accesses.

With the British/Western view that oil was the key element to both military power, and global financial dominance, the Ottoman situation was *not* going to remain; hence WWI was started, finished quickly (just 4 years), and The Ottoman territories were seized.

Historians give all sorts of lame reasons for WWI's propagation, but historians are mostly puppets, wittingly, and unwittingly churning out histories of pure propaganda. Looking back from our advanced time, the seizing of the Middle East oil ring was clearly WWI's primary goal, but clever deception was used to fool the public (and historians) into thinking otherwise.

The seizure of the Ottoman Territories has given, (and continues to give) the West an immense and

---

6. *Spingola. The Power Elite Playbook*

continuous torrent of super-wealth and global dominance.

The first British problem in the seized Ottoman Mideast however, was 'Arabs'.

After conquering the Middle East, British control of the ethnic populations was handled with brutality. After WWI, Winston Spencer Churchill was annoyed by the soft 'squeamishness' of the British establishment at the using of the time's cruelest weapon of mass destruction (nerve gas) against 'non-compliant' Iraqi Kurds, saying: "I am strongly in favor of using poisoned gas against uncivilized tribes. The moral effect should be good, and it would spread a lively terror."[7]

There was no terrorism then because any Arab uprising was simply crushed.

Back then, no justification to the Western public for British presence in the region was necessary. Ever since the invention of bomber aircraft, the 'West' has been randomly pulverizing Middle Easter civilian populations to 'keep them civilized'.

Call me crazy, but I'm guessing that this has contributed to their ingrained dislike for Westerners.

The British attitude of domination, cruelty, and violence for the purposes of controlling Middle East oil was considered to be fine at the time; not an eyelid was battered - it was just the way it was then.

But has anything changed today?

Well, of course, much has changed socially and psychologically in Western culture; people don't tolerate such a lack of inhumanity and violence - do they?

One certain change is that Governments can't be

---

7. *Spingola. The Power Elite Playbook*

seen to use the cruel tactics of yesteryear, but the Middle Eastern region still needs to be 'controlled'.

This is where deception becomes necessary.

A foggy confusion created for public consumption blurs the reality, and allows our government/corporate oil machine to do what is necessary to maintain their interests. Mideast oil flow *must* be controlled. Control the flow control the price is the motto of big oil. Slow the flow, raise the price.

If it were not for today's 'rise of terrorist groups', what justification for pre-emptive invasions and occupation of Mideast countries would we have?

Don't misunderstand me here - I am ***not*** saying terrorist groups don't exist, I am saying the opposite - they certainly exist, and they are brainwashed, cruel, violent, and dangerous - but are they 'allowed' to exist, and more importantly, to gain strength in order to provide justification for Western presence in the region? This is a relevant question - and a question which we must face and examine if we are to be truly objective - if we are to know reality.

At present it appears the Middle East is 'out of control', and in a sense it is, and in another sense - it is not. We shall clarify this 'chaos paradox' as we continue.

Once again I am no apologist for terrorism; but one must ask: has Mideast terrorism evolved naturally, predictably, and expectedly, because of specific, near perfect conditions? Alas, we are getting ahead of ourselves here.

WWII saw a shift in global power.

Japan seized French and British colonies. The British Empire was weakened. World boarders were again redrawn.

WWII's North Africa Desert War was fought for one reason: to gain control of the Middle East's oil fields (primarily in Iraq).

Hitler wanted the Iraq oil fields. Britain held them. Oil and petroleum were the keys to winning WWII, and in winning the Desert War, the Allies secured a vital victory.

WWII's end in 1945 however, saw the emergence of the United States as the new ruler of the Empire; the British would recede, and America's new enemy would be the communist, Stalinist, Soviet Union.[8]

The Promised Land

Israel has a long history of violent transition, much of which comes from biblical record.

Arabs conquered the region of Palaestina from the Greco-Roman Byzantine Empire in 635CE.[9]

Referred to in Arabic as South Assyria, it remained a Muslim country for the next 1300 years. In 1516, the region came under the umbrella of the Turkish or Ottoman Empire, until conquered by the British Empire as a result of World War One.[10]

The British renamed the region The British Mandate of Palestine.[11]

Palestine is not an Arab name; the Byzantine Empire renamed the region's provinces Palaestina Prima, and Palestina Secunda, in the year 614CE.[12]

---

8. Noam Chomsky. *Power & Terror in Our Times*
9. Moshe. *A History of Palestine, pgs634–1099. Cambridge University Press.*
10. Ibid
11. Ibid
12. Ibid

May 14, 1948, saw the re-formalization of the state of Israel.[13]

As per biblical scripture, Zionist Jews, disaffected by WWII, flooded the holy-land.[14] *They* were the chosen ones, the rightful inheritors of Israel and the new Jewish state.

But from his new capital city of Tel Aviv, David Ben Gurion, Israel's first Prime Minster, had two immediate problems:

1) What to do with the millions of Palestinian Arabs inhabiting the holy-land? And;

2) How to defend against an obvious and likely Arab uprising when the Palestinians were driven out?

Noam Chomsky points out in his complete work on the history of the Israeli/Arab conflict, *Fateful Triangle,* that: Israeli leaders, believing the Palestinians to be nomadic, assumed they would see the writing on the wall and simply 'move on', to Jordan or Syria or Iran.[15]

The Arabs, as it turns out, did see the writing on the wall, and 1948 saw the first Arab/ Israeli war. Five Arab states joined to fight a war of independence against the seizure of their land and the formation of Israel. It was a mistake that would reverberate through the coming decades.

As a result of the 1948 war, the State of Israel retained the area that the UN General Assembly Resolution

---

13. wikipedia. David Ben Gurion

14. Biblical scripture relating to Zionism, not of course, WWII

15. Taken from, Noam Chomsky. Fateful Triangle: The United States, Israel, and the Palestinians

181 had recommended for the proposed Jewish state and also took control of almost 60% of the area allocated for the proposed Arab state, including the Jaffa, Lydda and Ramle area, Galilee, some parts of the Negev desert, West Jerusalem, and territories in the West Bank.[16] (emphasis added)

The Egyptian military took control of Gaza.

No Arab Palestinian state was created, as was previously proposed. It is this fact that underlies all future tensions between Palestinians and Israel. So why did Israel seize the land assigned to a Palestinian State? Certainly punishment for attacking Israel would be one reason, but Ben Gurion's goal appeared to be to drive the Arabs out altogether, claiming the entire territory for the chosen people (as he saw it according to Biblical scripture), despite being the large Arab population's home for some 1300 years prior. Since then Israel has, at all costs, avoided the 'two state solution'. They just want the Arabs gone.

The British and Israeli treatment of the Palestinian people during the 1948 formation of Israel, such as driving them onto 'reservations', denying them access to their land, controlling their supply of water and food, embargoing and blockading them in a bully style take-over, triggered the first anti Western mindsets in the Arab world. One finds it particularly hard to blame them, or more accurately, one would *expect* some kind of fight-back from the disaffected indigenous peoples.

The 1948 Arab attack against their new overlords, backfired and has put them in a position with few options since.

---

16. *Taken from, Cragg (1997) pgs 57 & 116.*

In 1949 all combatant states signed the 1949 Armistice Agreements.

The conflict caused significant demographic upheaval. Around 700,000 Palestinian Arabs fled from the state of Israel as Palestinian refugees.[17] Around 700,000 Jews immigrated to Israel with one third of them having fled from their previous [Muslim] countries of residence in the Middle East.[18]

The Palestinian desire for a fair deal, or a two state solution has triggered an anti-Israel and anti-American mindset; the U.S. of course, providing *all* Israel's military arms, and millions in defense funding.[19]

What else did we expect? Palestinian dissent happened naturally.

The rise of IS however, would not happen naturally. The rise of IS would require a bizarre mix of extreme and special circumstances, all of which we will certainly cover.

---

17. Morris. The Birth of the Palestinian Refugee Problem Revisited
18. Ibid
19. Chomsky. Power & Terror in Our Times

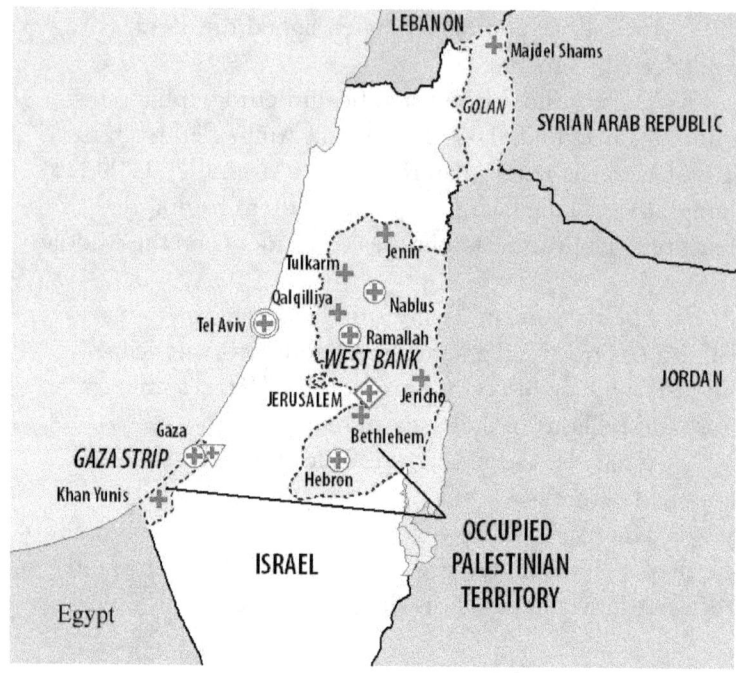

Israel. The grey areas within Israel; Gaza, West Bank, & Golan, being allocated to Palestinians

U.S. Academics tend to either fervently support Israel, or fervently support Palestinians. For me, neither position provides the facts to form a picture of reality, so in this case, most of our academics are useless. The Israel/Palestine topic is so emotive that the facts are both skewed and ignored to justify one's position in backing one side or the other.

Sekulow, in *The Rise of ISIS,* lists Hamas' atrocities (of which there are many) without considering the original conditions leading to their mindset. Sekulow omits all Israeli atrocities, of which there are many; and he leaves out key facts where Israeli actions have triggered a Hamas response. He skews the truth and is therefore (to me) useless. He is not useless however, to those with interests in Israeli dominance.

Note here that Hamas is and was democratically elected as the governing body of Gaza, by a proper *democratic* election process.

Noam Chomsky takes the direct opposite stance to Sekulow. Chomsky points out all Israel's atrocities against Palestinians, but omits atrocities by Hamas. Chomsky's opinions are formed through humanitarian thinking. Chomsky was one of the first to protest the Vietnam War on humanitarian grounds, and suffered cruel ridicule for his 'squeamish' attitude.

Sekulow, of course, believes that the Jews are right to do whatever they see fit in the 'holyland', because the bible says so; including wiping out Muslim Arabs.

So the Jewish (politically) want to wipe out the Palestinians; and the Palestinians (politically) want to wipe out the Jews (an impossibility of course, as they have no military ability to stand against the American backed Israeli Defense Force, or the IDF).

So the Arab/Israeli situation sits in stalemate, with no solution foreseeable.

With the breakup of Syria and Iraq, and a lawless anarchy giving rise to psychopathic groups of 'terrorists' - terrorists armed and funded by both U.S. and Saudi Arabian interests - Israel's Northern boarder appears threatened.

IS are certainly motivated by what they see as Israel's cruel occupation of the Palestinians, but this has not triggered their call to arms.

The Israeli question is: can this rag-tag band of crazies really threaten the might of the IDF?

The answer is no.

Israel is a 'tweeted' IS target, but it is simply not big enough, or well armed enough to go toe-to-toe with one of the biggest, complete defense forces in the world.

IS can't even threaten the Kurds on the Syrian/Turkish boarder; they simply don't have the numbers or the firepower.

Returning to Israel, we can see a clear counter-intelligence deception in play; a deception against us.

The U.S. gives $8,500,000 per day in Military aid to Israel.[20] The U.S. backs and needs Israel to be strong in the region.

The U.S. political machine does not want its citizens sympathizing with Palestinians; so we are manipulated in a variety of ways to see Palestinians as 'terrorists', and Israelis as non-terrorists; when in reality, they are both as bad as each other.

They are happy for your reality to be 'blurred' if it suits them politically or financially; and this is why things

---

20. *The American Empire Project*

appear 'foggy', and why we need to keep abreast of deception designed for us.

An Overview of the Middle Eastern Situation

Before we kick on and start tackling the big questions, a basic understanding of the alliances and structures of the Muslim Middle East is needed.

OPEC: Or the Organization of Petroleum Exporting Countries, is an intergovernmental organization formed in 1960. Current member countries of the Middle East are:

> UAE: 2.7 million Barrels per day.
> Kuwait: 2.5 million bpd
> Qatar: 1.2 million bpd
> Iran: 4.2 million bpd
> Iraq: 3.2 million bpd
> Saudi Arabia: 8.8 million bpd

African members are:

> Libya: 2.2 million bpd
> Nigeria: 2.2 million bpd
> Algeria: 2.1 million bpd
> Angola: 1.9 million bpd

South American members are:

> Ecuador: 485, 000 bpd
> Venezuela: 2.4 million bpd[21]

Barrel per day outputs ***do not*** reflect the size of a country's oil reservoirs. OPEC puts quota limits on each country in

---

21. OPEC, *wikipedia*

order to control the flow and pricing, and to prevent gluts. When a country goes 'rogue', and exceeds limits, a variety of options exist to return that 'rogue' to compliance; U.S. Military/CIA intervention included.

Hamas: Founded in 1987 and evolving from The Muslim Brotherhood, Hamas was and is a terrorist group in the eyes of the intelligence apparatus of Israel, The United Kingdom, The United States of America, The European Union, Australia, New Zealand, Canada, and Egypt.

Hamas is not considered a terrorist organization by Russia, China, Iran, or Turkey.[22]

> [In] the January 2006 Palestinian parliamentary elections, Hamas won a decisive majority in the Palestinian Parliament, defeating the PLO-affiliated[sic] Fatah Party.[23] (of the West Bank).

Hamas preaches Sunni Islam. Their ideological goal is for Palestinian self-determination.

Hamas' 1988 charter states that Hamas [s]trives to raise the banner of Allah over every inch of Palestine; and that, [I]srael will exist and will continue to exist until Islam will obliterate it, just as it obliterated others before it. And; [U]nder the wing of Islam, it is possible for the followers of the three religions, Islam, Christianity and Judaism, to coexist in peace and quiet with each other.[24]

Palestine and Israel are not oil producing countries. The U.S. however gives Israel billions in 'aid'.

---

22. *wikipedia: Hamas*
23. *BBC News, 26/1/2006, Who are Hamas?*
24. *Hamas Covenant, 1988 version*

Hamas is violently opposed to Israel's formation and their blockade of Palestine. (Palestine no longer exists as a country.)

Hamas' military strength consists of suicide bombers, and SUV mounted rocket launchers.

The goal of Hamas' terror attacks against Israeli civilians is to force the Palestinian plight into Western thinking, vis-à-vis the Viet Cong throughout the Vietnam War.

Sunni and Shia Muslims: Sunni Islam is Islam's largest branch taking in 89% of the world's Muslim population.[25] It is a strict, orthodox version of the Islamic religion. Shia Muslims are the minority Islamic group (11%).

Shia Muslims however, are the majority in both Iran and Iraq.[26]

In religious terms, the Sunni/Shia split hinges on a dispute dating back to the death of the prophet Muhammad. The dispute is over who will succeed the prophet as the Caliph, or the righteous religious ruler of the Caliphate.

Focusing *only* on the Middle East, it appears that human nature and human savagery have seeped into the Islamic psyche, and that this religious difference is simply used to justify corrupt regional and political actions within Syria and Iraq, including murder, violence, power, control, and conquest.

Currently, Muslim extremists and terrorists call themselves Sunni Muslims; although virtually all of their violent actions are unlawful under Sunni religious law.

---

25. *Pew Research Centre: Mapping the Global Muslim Population*
26. *Ibid*

Kurds: The Kurdish population of almost 30 million consists predominantly of Sunni Muslims. They have no country of their own, but occupy the boarder fringes of Turkey/Syria, Iraq/Syria, Iraq/Turkey, and Iraq/Iran.[27] These areas are referred to as Kurdistan, although it is not an official country.

Within these areas the Kurds pump crude oil, and reportedly, Iran refines this Kurdish crude and sells it for them on the black-market.[28]

Despite their Iranian lineage, Iran keeps these Kurds in line with occasional artillery shelling. And this type of brutal control is all they know. In the Mideast, if you're naughty you'll get bombed. This is their reality, but it is a reality that we simply cannot grasp.

We simply don't understand what that's like.

Like the Palestinians, the Kurds want their own state.

The Kurdish Military arm, the Peshmerga, recently took control of the Iraqi oil town of Kirkuk; but as per U.S. Mideast doctrine, the U.S. is now arming and training the Peshmerga, using them to fight IS in Iraq.

Historically, the U.S. system has been to arm and train various Mideast factions in order to stem one uprising or another, and what always happens is this: when the U.S. or CIA regional operatives no longer need said group and pull support, leaving them to their fate, the survivors of said group gains a hatred for *America*.

---

27. *The official CIA Fact-book, and; Mackenzie. The Origin of Kurdish: Transactions of Philological Society, pgs 68–86*
28. *Van Buren. Seven Worst Case Scenarios in the Battle with the Islamic State (10.16.2014)*

This is exactly what is happening with Iraqi Kurds right now, in October of 2014. This arming and dropping, supporting then killing, has happened numerous times since 1945, and the U.S. imperial handover.

The danger is this: the Kurds, desperate for a state of their own, hungry for greater income for their people, horrifically disaffected, and armed to the teeth by the U.S. could potentially become the next 'IS'. (or something similar)

Later we will examine why the U.S. administration is not even slightly worried by this possibility.

Turkey: Turkey is a U.S. client state with a big, modern, and powerful military (in conventional terms).

The U.S. funds the Turks to smash their Kurdish dissidents on the Syrian boarder and in Southern Turkey.

Now the U.S. is also funding the Kurds to fight IS in Syria and Iraq.

The U.S. always provides air-power to the secular group it currently supports via drones and fighter-bombers. Air-power is key in the Mideast, because in can't be stopped; can be used any time and for any length of time; and is perfect for corralling a group, in a 'Limited war' style.

Limited war, as per the Vietnam Blueprint, is designed to control an area whilst keeping the weaker enemy force 'in the game'.

Why keep the weaker enemy force in the game?

Because while the region is embroiled in civil war, and full of terrorist cells, the U.S. Empire can justify its presence in the region.

The U.S. needs to be in the Mideast to oversee and control the flow of oil; because big oil owns the U.S. government. Compliant Third World dictators have to be installed in Mideast countries, but these Third World dictators often have the nasty habit of selling their oil on the black market, or worse, wanting to flood the market. It is at this point in a Third World dictator's existence, that he must be removed.

Also consider this: the current U.S. operations in Iraq siphons 10 million dollar per day; taken from the taxpaying public and given to the Military Industrial Complex.

Any rebuilding programs or infrastructure repair projects afterwards work the same way.

Syria: With Turkey and the Kurds to the North, and Israel's mighty IDF to the South, Bashar Al Assad's Syria is pinched.

IS want to control the region of Syria and Iraq to create the new Islamic State Caliphate, taking the population back into the dark-ages in the same way the Taliban destroyed Afghanistan.

Boys, girls, women, and children opposed to IS's draconian takeover are prepared to stand and fight Islamic State militants. Yet we in the West are led to believe that ISIS, (a relatively small rag-tag militia, holding only small arms) poses a 9/11 type terrorist threat to the United States.

IS is evil. IS uses social media (like twitter) to spread fear.

But does IS pose a threat to Turkey? No.

Does IS pose a threat the Israel? No.

In regards to America, IS would relish the chance to effect a terrorist attack on American soil - IS has the will, but by no way the means.

Could U.S. forces wipeout IS in the Mideast?

The question is: do they want to?

One thing is certain; when the U.S. decides to, they can and will remove IS.

At this point, it is interesting to note that The Moroccan Times, along with several Mideast news agencies, has reported that Chechen President, Ramzan Kadyrov, has made the statement that ISIL's (IS's) terrorist leader, Abu Bakr al-Baghdadi, is a CIA plant.

Kadyrov said: "Baghdadi should take off his mask and declare loudly and clearly that he is a CIA agent, that he has been recruited." Adding: "They (IS) are Shaitans (devils) and their sole obsession is to grab as much money as they can lay hands on. ***They are acting on orders from the West and deliberately exterminating Muslims.***"emphasis added

This can also be seen at Kadyrov's facebook page.

It is certainly possible, and certainly not the first time that the CIA has been caught operating in this way. British SAS soldiers have been captured previously in Iraq, dressed as insurgents and inciting violence.

Syria's Assad, supported by Iran and therefore Russia, was according to Vladimir Putin, "stabilizing the region".

If Kadyrov's claim is true, and I'm not saying it is, why would the U.S. want to 'destabilize' a region that it wants to control?

According to Professor Noam Chomsky, the system inherited by the U.S. from the British, goes like this: to control the Mideast oil region, install weak U.S. puppet governments and pay them and support them militarily. If an uprising threatens the U.S. friendly regime, as they invariably will, the U.S. will supply the means to crush them.

It is a fact however, that these Muslim rebel groups are also, from time-to-time, armed and funded by CIA operatives. This is done for two reasons:

1) To use rebel groups to remove non-compliant regimes, whist giving the CIA plausible deniability, and;

2) To *de*-stabilize.
So why de-stabilize the Mideast?
OPEC countries and the regions around them cannot be allowed to form more advanced, technological, or educated societies. This would interfere with or even collapse U.S. control over the Mideast oil ring. Destabilization, or more accurately - civil war - ensures this will never happen.

The CIA created a civil war in Vietnam.

The CIA created a civil war in Afghanistan.

The CIA flooded both Vietnam and Afghanistan with massive amounts of small arms; in Vietnam's case, enough for WWII's planned U.S. invasion of Japan, not required due to the late arrival of two atomic bombs.[29] These arms were funneled through Ho Chi Minh to the North Vietnamese Army (NVA), whom the U.S. would eventually be fighting in a protracted ten year war.

The same is true for Afghanistan, Al Qaeda, and the Taliban. The same is also true for Syria and the Islamic State. Will the same be true for the Kurds?

The Obama administration has armed these Syrian

---

29. *Marshal Douglas Smith. Black Gold Hot Gold*

Rebels *(for free)*, while Russia has sold the Syrian government all of its weapons.

Western interests, including Turkey and Saudi Arabia, want to remove the non-compliant, (Mideast stabilizing), Bashar Al-Assad from power in Syria. They have to be cunning though, because it is said that Russia supports Assad.

The Jihadists in the region, (Al Qaeda and IS), want to knock out any and all U.S. friendly regimes, and possibly, *any* regimes at all. Without U.S. or Israeli intervention, IS could take control of Syria and/or Iraq.

It appears, as we will 'study' later, that the U.S. is happy to corral IS, letting them run wild, albeit within a tightly controlled area, creating a bloody civil war and regressing the region back into the dark-ages.

The CIA is using local Islamic Jihadist factions to do two things:

> 1) The CIA arms Syrian rebels hoping to topple and remove Assad, so as a compliant dictator can be installed, (they don't mind that these rebels fight Assad alongside IS, and they don't mind that weapons fall into IS hands. And;

> 2) They arm and use Muslim groups such as the Kurds to corral IS, push them out of Kurdistan and Iraq, and back on to Assad. Once IS topple Assad and fulfill other goals, the U.S. will quickly remove them.

Interestingly the current propaganda line on IS from the Western political realm is: "to *slowly degrade* and push them (IS) back".

I think the CIA means to keep them in the game, and turn them on Assad, grabbing money and arms to effect the overthrow as they go.

Okay, I think it's time we step back and take a look at the Cold War; and more to the point, the Cold War's influence on the current Middle Eastern situation.

2

Out in the Cold

The Cold War is one of the most interesting and fascinating periods of history; (to me it is the most fascinating). This is because the Cold War is really a montage of deceptions, cleverly and desperately interwoven to achieve U.S. global domination whilst simultaneously appearing moral and righteous.

The Cold War was/is corporate driven.

The Cold War had/has many goals including but not limited to:

1) 1945: the acquisition of Nazi high technology.[30]

2) The development of this technology for global domination. (Nuclear weapons; Scalar Weapons; Non fossil fuel based propulsion systems for air/space travel).[31]

3) The use of a deception montage to cover the existence of high technologies. (Possibly alternative propulsion/ discoid UFO spacecraft).[32]

---

30. *Farrell. Reich of the Black Sun*
31. *Ibid*
32. *Ibid*

4) The creation and advancement of 'obsolete' and/or oil dependent technologies, so as to cover 'hidden', more advanced technologies; and to conceal manmade UFO technology at all costs.[33]

5) To dominate the world's oil supply and ensure the world's dependence on oil - oil being an already obsolete technology.

6) To do so by creating a climate of 'false fear'.

7) To use this 'false fear' to launch highly profitable pre-emptive wars (in oil rich regions).

8) To expand WWII's massive Military Industrial Complex into areas of low-tech, but highly profitable weapons and arms production to prosecute long, drawn out occupations of countries. i.e: Vietnam (oil) Afghanistan One (oil) Iraq One (oil) South America (oil) Yugoslavia (oil) Afghanistan Two (oil) Iraq Two (oil).[34]

9) To somehow control the indigenous populations in oil producing regions; especially those of the Middle East, the Empires largest and most profitable oil region.[35]

At WWII's death, Soviet Russia and The U.S. squabbled and fought for control and possession of Nazi secret technology, scientists, and engineers.[36]

---

33. *Lyne. Pentagon Aliens*
34. *Spingola. The Power Elite Playbook*
35. *Chomsky. Fateful Triangle: The United States, Israel, and the Palestinians*
36. *Farrell. Reich of the Black Son*

The U.S. seized and took Nazi scientists in all weaponizable fields back stateside (illegally) during operations *Alsos* and *Paperclip*, triggering the first post war deception against her own taxpaying public.[37]

The race with Soviet Russia was on for nuclear weapons, and space domination. Fear of nuclear annihilation was all consuming. The Vietnam War was justified at the time by Defense Secretary Robert McNamara and President Lyndon Johnson, as being critical to stop the global spread of Soviet communism. They constantly reinforced the danger of the 'domino effect', where if one country fell to communism, the next would fall in an unstoppable chain-reaction – a red tide threatening the free world.

Blueprint Vietnam: The Limited War Model

The first and most important Cold War consideration when unweaving the Vietnam War deception montage is to understand the political mindset, and the operational psychology of the Pentagon and the Joint Chiefs of Staff (JCS) preceding hostilities circa 1964. I say circa 1964 because the U.S. (in the form of the CIA), was conducting covert military operations in Indochina[38] prior to the Tonkin Resolution, a congressional authorization for military action given in response to a 1964 attack by a North Vietnamese

---

37. *Ibid*

38. *Laos, Cambodia, and Vietnam; the French loosing Indochina as a colony in 1954 after military defeat by Ho Chi Minh's, Viet Minh at Diem Bin Phu*

Navy patrol boat against two U.S. warships in the Gulf of Tonkin. The validity of the attacks however, hangs in question.[39]

The first psychological insight comes from the Operation Northwoods briefing documents.

Painstakingly thought-out and composed by the Joint Chiefs of Staff and their Pentagon advisors, the 14 page Operation Northwoods document was presented to Defense Secretary McNamara on March 13, 1962.[40]

> [O]peration Northwoods' purpose was to gain public support for a planned military invasion of Cuba. The methods and/or 'options' outlined in detail in the Operation Northwoods briefing documents called for innocent civilians to be shot on American streets, the sinking of Cuban refugee boats, and self-inflicted terrorism inside Washington D.C and/or Miami. Other Northwoods options included self-inflicted vehicle and building bombings, sabotaging NASA rockets, and airliner hijackings - all of which people could be 'framed for', while laying the ultimate blame on Cuba's Fidel Castro.[41]

As I pointed out in *A Time for Deception,* The JCS terror plan of 1962 was rejected by J.F. Kennedy, and was not implemented under his Presidency - but on November 22, 1963, he was of course, assassinated.

Just take this in for a second: in 1962, the JCS felt it acceptable to maim and kill American citizens and other

---

39. There were two alleged NVN attacks; August 2nd & 4th. An FOIA NSA document stated the attack on the 4th did not happen.

40. FOIA: Operation Northwoods Briefing Document (Facsimile)

41. Stone. A Time for Deception, pg81

innocent civilians in order to justify a military attack on Cuba – they were going to keep it all a secret though.

In *A Time for Deception* I ask the obvious: was this idea of *self-inflicted* American terrorism proposed by the JCS revived after Kennedy's death by the new President, Lyndon. B. Johnson?

I have shown, as have others, that the Gulf of Tonkin Incident used to justify the 10 plus year military invasion (and destruction) of Vietnam, was a 'noble lie', necessary according to the Joint Chiefs to rein in communism during the Cold War climate of fear.

But was that all? Was there an ulterior motive?

Our natural desire to reduce fear and make the world safe for our children drove the common man to want to go to Vietnam and 'kill communists'.

There were very few Vietnamese who even understood the meaning of communism then. Ho Chi Minh was one man who did; a man (like Osama Bin Laden after him) who was recently on the American/CIA payroll).[42]

What am I saying here? Well, I'm asking: did the CIA use Ho Chi Minh to orchestrate and drive a 'communist uprising' in Vietnam; an uprising that would sustain a prolonged U.S. occupation? And does this situation sound similar to Osama Bin Laden's Al Qaeda; armed, supplied, and driven by the CIA to fight Soviet Russia to the very last Afghan, in 1979? Once again I've gotten ahead of myself.

What I can say at this point is that the Vietnam War and its methods clearly became the 'blueprint' model for invading and occupying a non compliant state in the

---

42. Stone. *The Cover of War research; interview with Hòng Nguyen*

'squeamish' age of morals and humanity.

Let's look at the facts:

1) LBJ used a 'false-flag' trigger to gain both congressional and public support for Invasion Vietnam. The NVN attack on USS Maddox and USS Turner Joy never happened, but were turned into convenient justifications, as per the Op Northwoods document, for a 10 year occupation.[43]

2) The Vietnam occupation had bizarre rules of engagement that bamboozled generals and kept the weaker NVA forces 'in the game', such as;

a) Not attacking SAM missile sites until fully operational.

b) Not pursuing NVA ground forces across the Cambodian boarder, giving them safe staging, and bail-out areas.

c) Limited war, and the bizarre nature of 'firebase' warfare, and ineffective 'search and destroy' operations; as opposed to conventional tactics.

d) The bizarre circumstance of requiring *all* tactical and battle plans to be approved by the UN Security Council, headed by ex *Soviet* General, Alexel Nesternko.[44] The question asked by U.S. Generals on the ground was: He's a communist, so is he passing our critical tactical information to his communist allies?

---

43. *Spingola. The Power Elite Playbook*
44. *United Nations Security Council Records*

Travis Stone

~~TOP SECRET SPECIAL HANDLING NOFORN~~

THE JOINT CHIEFS OF STAFF
WASHINGTON 13, D.C.

UNCLASSIFIED

13 March 1962

MEMORANDUM FOR THE SECRETARY OF DEFENSE

Subject: Justification for US Military Intervention in Cuba (TS)

1. The Joint Chiefs of Staff have considered the attached Memorandum for the Chief of Operations, Cuba Project, which responds to a request of that office for brief but precise description of pretexts which would provide justification for US military intervention in Cuba.

2. The Joint Chiefs of Staff recommend that the proposed memorandum be forwarded as a preliminary submission suitable for planning purposes. It is assumed that there will be similar submissions from other agencies and that these inputs will be used as a basis for developing a time-phased plan. Individual projects can then be considered on a case-by-case basis.

3. Further, it is assumed that a single agency will be given the primary responsibility for developing military and para-military aspects of the basic plan. It is recommended that this responsibility for both overt and covert military operations be assigned the Joint Chiefs of Staff.

For the Joint Chiefs of Staff:

SYSTEMATICALLY REVIEWED
BY JCS ON ___ May 84
CLASSIFICATION CONTINUED

L. L. LEMNITZER
Chairman
Joint Chiefs of Staff

1 Enclosure
Memo for Chief of Operations, Cuba Project   EXCLUDED FROM GDS

> EXCLUDED FROM AUTOMATIC
> REGRADING: DOD DIR 5200.10
> DOES NOT APPLY

~~TOP SECRET SPECIAL HANDLING NOFORN~~

Page 1 of the 14 page Operation Northwoods briefing document

3) The Vietnam War's incredibly high consumption of bullets and bombs made huge money for the arms manufacturing companies of America's Military Industrial Alliance. All of the 350-900 billion dollars spent on the ten year Vietnam War was loaned through the Federal Reserve System [the government doesn't hold a supply of cash for wars]. Tax-take pays the interest on the loans. The companies forming the Military/ Industrial supply chain made a killing from a taxpayer funded money conversion.[45]

4) The Vietnam War had a massive oil component, integral to the war's timetable and sequence of events, such as;

a) Intimate knowledge of President Herbert Hoover's 1920 oil survey, which estimated Vietnam's offshore oil reserve to be one of the world's largest.

b) A lengthy and precise survey, using ship based echo sounding in the South China Sea along Vietnam's Eastern coast was conducted during the war's duration - ending around the same time as U.S. military withdrawal.

c) This highly detailed survey had to be kept secret from the French and Chinese, but particularly the French.

d) After Soviet collapse circa 1991, U.S. oil companies acquired lucrative drilling contracts in

---

45. Stone. *A Time for Deception, pg91*

the area surveyed during the Vietnam War.[46]

5) The French, an American 'ally', ran Vietnam as a profit making export colony prior to military defeat by the Vietnamese in 1954. But the plethora of weapons used by Ho Chi Minh's Viet Minh army to beat the French were supplied (for Ho's later 'good will') by the U.S.[47]

This means the U.S. committed a blatant act of war against an ally. Why would they do this?

Of course, to control the region in order to get control of "one of the planet's largest undersea oil stocks", the French had to be removed. This means;

6) The CIA used and employed Ho Chi Minh to do its dirty work in North Vietnam: removing the French, destabilizing the region; recruiting key figures; and then creating an uprising, whilst simultaneously installing a U.S. 'friendly' puppet government in South Vietnam.

The split in the country, North communist and South not, may have occurred naturally (I personally doubt it though), but this 'split' was critical if there was to be a 'war', for without two 'sides', there could be no 'fight'.

The psychological system unleashed on the Western psyche at this time was: Fear (of communist takeover); Trigger (NVN Patrol boat attack); Revenge/patriotism; Invasion; Occupation.

---

46. *Marshall Douglas Smith. Black Gold Hot Gold*
47. *Ibid*

The outcome:

1) A compliant Vietnam.

2) Huge profit to the Military Industrial Complex and the Federal Reserve.

3) Detailed knowledge of Vietnam's undersea oil stocks, and;

3) Later control of the flow of Vietnam's. (Control the flow control the price).

4) A tested and proven, flexible blueprint for a country's pre-emptive invasion and occupation.

When the Vietnam blueprint is laid over the *War on Terror's* invasion of Iraq, the pattern is clear. The Deception is difficult to hide.

Hence it is not only important for the American Empire to run a network of disinformation and deception around pre-emptive wars and oil occupations, but they must also breed both fear and morality into the populations psyche.

Sucked In: The Cold War Vacuum

Long before the Soviet invasion of Afghanistan on December 24, 1979, the CIA was *already* in country, forming, arming, and training a group of radical Muslims, later called the Mujahideen.[48]

---

48. *Documentary: Our Own Private Bin Laden*

President Jimmy Carter signed the first official directive for *secret* aid to the Mujahideen on July 3, 1979.[49] Six months before the Soviet Invasion.

The CIA used a well connected, wealthy, and enigmatic Saudi Arabian to organize and lead the Mujahideen; Osama Bin Laden.

Zbigniew Brzezinski, (National Security Advisor to President Carter, and later counselor to Lyndon Johnson), was instrumental in the strategy behind the 1979-89 Soviet/Afghan War.[50]

Brzezinski was the brains of this operation, which had goals far wider than the obvious maiming of the Soviet Military.

Brzezinski ensured a large, well armed, well supported, and well trained *Jihadist* Mujahideen was ready for war *before* he began luring the Soviet Military toward them.[51] All this was done in secret and masked by deception plans.

We were told that military aid to the Mujahideen was a necessary response to Soviet Invasion - when the CIA had been preparing the Mujahideen for months. We were told that the Soviet Invasion of Afghanistan was: "The biggest threat to peace since WWII".[52]

Schools teaching a new form of 'radical Islamic Jihad' were set up in Afghanistan by the CIA for the sole purpose of inflaming a very impressionable group of young men into fighting the Soviets by means of Jihad, or holy war against the Soviet Union. Another word for this is

---

49. *Documentary: Our Own Private Bin Laden*
50. *Ibid*
51. *Ibid*
52. *Ibid*

brainwashing.

Yes, we created these people. But the reality is much worse.

Brzezinski knew that once in Jihad mode, these Muslims would never give up. Most political experts on the subject say that to realize his dreams, Brzezinski was prepared to fight the Soviets to the very last Muslim.

I think it was more calculated.

As we will see, basic tactical deception planning is laid down for decades in advance – in regards to the supposedly mighty Soviet Union, I think their time had simply come to be 'removed' from center stage.

Brzezinski planned and lured the Soviet Union into an un-winnable, protracted ten year war against his Mujahideen, assisting in weakening the Soviet Military, and eventually resulting in the Soviet Union's collapse (in 1991).[53]

The same mighty and powerful Soviet Union we were taught to fear by mass media bombardment, was essentially destroyed by a U.S. funded group of around 35,000 radical Islamist warriors from 30 odd Muslim countries.

The CIA created an Afghani Jihad, inflaming it into a global war against the Soviet Union. In doing so however, they armed, organized, and created the first Islamic Jihad Armies. "A militant Islamic network was created by the CIA."[54]

When asked if he regretted giving arms and [military] advice to the world's future terrorists, Brzezinski said: "What is most important to the history of the world - the Taliban

---

53. *Ibid*
54. *Zbigniew Brzezinski. Le Nouvel Observeteur, 1998*

or the collapse of the Soviet Empire? Some stirred up Muslims or the liberation of Central Europe and the end of the Cold War?"[55]

Note that Brzezinski clearly did not believe that such terror groups had any ability to attack or pose a military threat to the West; and as we will see, they don't.

Brzezinski firmly and aggressively defends the plan that put Afghan men and boys through a Soviet meat-grinder in order to bring about his defeat of the USSR; but Brzezinski can't deny the fact that it was all pre-planned. He can't deny the fact that the CIA flooded literally billions of dollars of 'laundered' money, from the corrupt bank, the BCCI, into Afghanistan, and allowed heroin, weighed by the metric ton, to be shipped out, bound for Western countries including the U.S.[56]

Nothing would stop them from removing the Soviet Union's influence from the Middle East oil ring.

In the documentary: *Our Own Private Bin Laden,* the interviewer asks Stansfield Turner (CIA director during the Soviet Afghan War) the following: "Is there a difference between killing in the name of Islam, and killing in the name of democracy?"

Turner went defensive; the question was too hard to answer, and the interviewer was told to not ask hard questions.

Noam Chomsky suggests that the U.S. has been engaged in active terrorism for years, listing throughout his extensive works, hundreds of occasions where 'we' have

---

55. *Ibid*
56. *Documentary: Our Own Private Bin Laden*

bombed and maimed civilians in clear acts of terrorism. He suggests that if we want to stop terrorism, we should firstly stop participating in it.[57]

Chomsky also suggests that all acts of violence are horrific, but our mindset is that it's okay when we do it to them, and it's terrorism when they do it to us.[58]

The Rise of Al Qaeda

Why did Al Qaeda and the Mujahideen turn from an Islamic Fundamentalist Jihad against the Soviet Union, to jihad against the West, in-particular, America?

It is *not* because they hate us for our freedom, or 'superior' way of life.

After that first Afghan War in 1989, Al Qaeda was simply a list of Muslim fighters, compiled by Bin Laden for a future call to arms.[59] That call to arms ironically, would be against those who created, funded, supplied, midwifed, and nursed it to life - The U.S.

The already 'fundamentalist' Al Qaeda declared Jihad on the U.S. for the following reasons:

> 1) When the defeated Soviets withdrew from Afghanistan, the U.S. simply packed up and left, leaving the Afghans to their pulverized, 'stone-age' fate.
>
> 2) Al Qaeda opposed the Israeli/American treatment

---

57. *Chomsky. Power and Terror in Our Times*
58. *Ibid*
59. *Documentary: Oil Factor*

of the Palestinians. This is fundamental for all Arab Muslims.

3) They opposed the system of U.S. Empire in the Middle East; a system of killing non-compliant although democratically elected leaders, and replacing them with U.S. puppets.

4) They opposed the CIA's system of feeding arms into the region to effect overthrows by triggering bloody civil wars.

5) They oppose U.S. domination of their country's oil production; believing that it's their land, so it is their oil to sell as they please.

6) They oppose the disparity in oil payments; where the U.S. was selling a barrel of oil for $130, the producing Mideast country was getting mere cents.

7) In Saudi Arabia, Bin Laden opposed the barrel price there too, around $20; much more than Mideast countries, but still far too disparate in Bin Laden's view.

8) In addition, the CIA instigated overthrow of Iran's Shah in 1979, and subsequent replacement with a puppet Ayatollah, triggered a (distinct and separate) wave of Islamic fundamentalism throughout Iran.

9) Essentially they all want their countries back; but don't they realize that they are ruled by an Empire?

So Al Qaeda arose from the rubble hell-bent on revenge; as did several other, independent and separate Islamic

Fundamentalist factions across the old Ottoman Empire, not under the control of Osama Bin Laden.

If the U.S. policy makers wanted to build, create, inflame, and turn Islamic Fundamentalism against them, they sure did everything possible to ensure it.

The question is: did the CIA orchestrate this situation to ensure unrest and civil war, keeping the Mideast in the 'stone-age' or the 'dark-age' so as to control OPEC and its neighbors?

> [T]he good lord didn't see fit to put oil and gas only where there are régimes friendly to the U.S. - but we go where the business is. ~ *Dick Cheney, U.S. Vice President, 2001-09* [60]

> [T]ake the profit out of warfare and there would be peace; take the profit out of illness and there would be health; take the profit out of addiction and there would be temperance. ~ *Deanna Spingola*

---

60. *Documentary: Our Own Private Bin Laden*

Part Two

The War of Terror

3

9/11

A Necessary Evil?

As Hitler's henchman, Herman Goring said: "The way to make a nation do everything you want is simply to tell them they are under attack."[61]

But did the American Empire go a step further, and actually make sure they *were* attacked; the fear of attack being real because it is real?

As will be discussed later, Middle Eastern terror groups, born in the stone-age conditions of Cold War Afghanistan, have never had the ability or the strength (they have the will and the intent) to conduct effective strike operations off-shore.

Both 9/11 and the 7/7 London subway attack were carried out by Al Qaeda, Osama Bin Laden's network of Islamic Jihadists; but were the perfect conditions 'created', where Al Qaeda felt they *could* pull off those attacks? Was the (continued) Saudi funding to Al Qaeda authorized by U.S. powers?

Did the 'Bush cartel' create these conditions so as to effect a horrific act of 'Islamic terrorism' on American soil, providing limitless justification to attack, invade, and occupy

---

61. *The History Channel. Conspiracy Files*

any Middle Eastern country required, for the foreseeable future?

If so, The War on Terror is a magnificently effective piece of counter-public deception, which (if true) works because it makes us deeply fear a terror attack in our own country; this is a deception nonetheless, straight out of Hitler's Nazi playbook.

A plethora of circumstantial evidence of this 9/11 false-flag operation has mounted up, but short of an admission, nothing will sway the belief to accept this idea. If 9/11 was an 'inside job', as they say, then the Bush cartel got away with it.

Hmm, something about 'creating' and 'studying' reality.

What interests me regarding the War on Terror is the way politicians lie through their teeth to justify and cover the *inconsistencies*. That which at face value seems justified, breaks down when major justifications are found to be lies.

No Intelligence

The U.S. Intelligence Community, a group of 10 major alphabet organizations, and totaling 17 intelligence organizations sucking 68 million dollars per year in operating costs, would certainly have known and worked out Al Qaeda's 9/11 plans. Although denial was the initial rhetorical tactic, too much evidence to the contrary forced a change of tack - to ignorance and dis-organization.

The following CIA memo, sent to the Immediate White House Situation Room in December of 1998, is entitled:

------PLANNING BY USAMA BIN LADEN
TO HIJACK U.S AIRPLANE; SUCESSFUL
CIRCUMVENTION OF SECURITY MEASURES IN
U.S. AIRPORT.

The un-blanked out parts of the document
state:

- - - - BIN LADEN WAS PLANNING TO
EXECUTE NEW OPERATIONS AGAINST UNITED
STATES (U.S.) TARGETS IN THE NEAR
FUTURE. PLANS TO HIJACK A U.S AIRCRAFT
WERE PROCEEDING WELL. TWO INDIVIDUALS
FROM THE RELEVANT OPERATIONAL TEAM IN
THE U.S. HAD SUCESSFULLY EVADED SECURITY
CHECKS DURING A TRIAL RUN AT 'NEW YORK
AIRPORT - - - BIN LADEN HOPED THAT THE
OPERATION WOULD BE IMPLEMENTED BEFORE
THE START OF RAMADAN.
- -
CIRA 20 DECEMBER.) THE OBJECTIVE OF THE
OPERATION IS TO OBTAIN THE RELEASE OF
BLIND SHAYKE 'UMAR AHMAD 'ABD AL-
((RAHMAN)), RAMZI ((YOUSEF)) AND
MUHAMMAD SADIQ ((ODEH)), A SUSPECT IN
THE BOMBING OF THE U.S. EMBASSY IN
NAIROBI, KENYA. - - - -
YOUSEF AND RAHMAN WERE CONVICTED OF THE
WORLD TRADE CENTER BOMBING IN NEW
YORK. [62](all spelling in the original)

---

62. *FOIA: National Security Archive. View online at:*
http://www2.gwu.edu/~nsarchiv/NSAEBB/NSAEBB381/

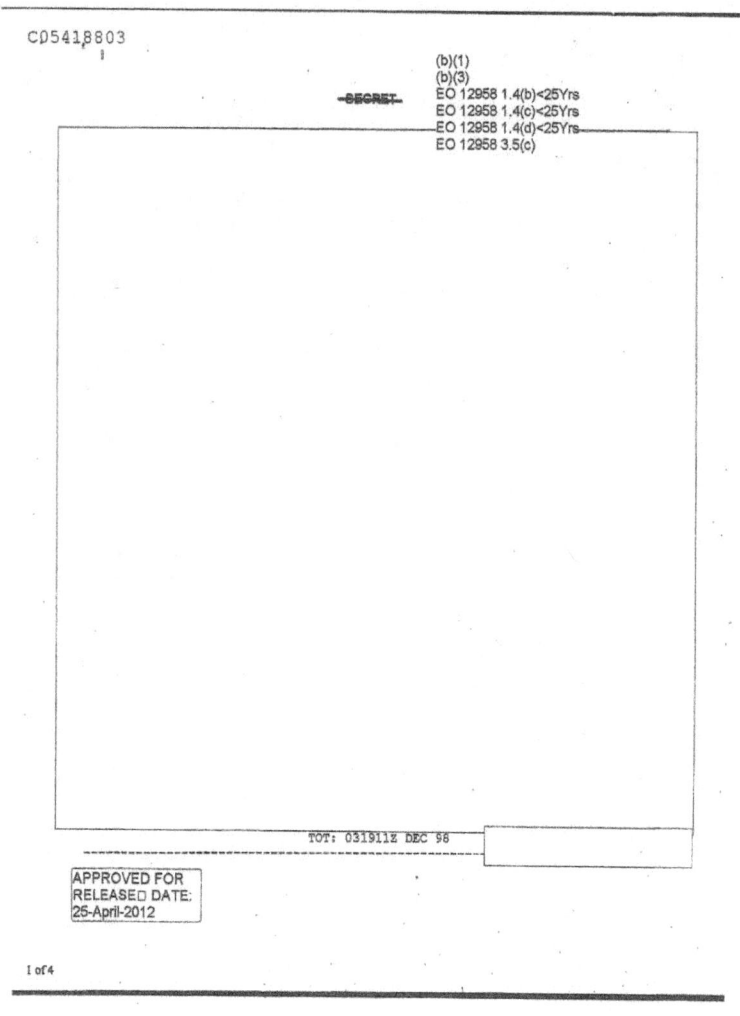

(b)(1)
(b)(3)
EO 12958 1.4(b)<25Yrs
EO 12958 1.4(c)<25Yrs
EO 12958 1.4(d)<25Yrs
EO 12958 3.5(c)

~~SECRET~~

TOT: 031911Z DEC 98

APPROVED FOR
RELEASED DATE:
25-April-2012

1 of 4

CQ5418803

~~S E C R E T~~

TO: IMMEDIATE WHITE HOUSE SITUATION ROOM,
SECSTATE WASEDC//INR//, DIA WASHINGTON DC, DA WASHINGTON DC,
ONI WASHINGTON DC, CNO WASHINGTON DC, CMC WASHINGTON DC,
CSAF WASHINGTON DC, DIRNSA, FEDERAL BUREAU OF INVESTIGATION,
SECRET SERVICE//ID//, DEPARTMENT OF JUSTICE WASH DC//OIPR//,
FAA NATIONAL HQ, DEPT OF TRANSPORTATION//S-60//,
USCINCTRANS INTEL CEN SCOTT AFB IL,
USCINCSOC INTEL OPS CEN MACDILL AFB

CENTRAL INTELLIGENCE AGENCY

WARNING: INFORMATION REPORT, NOT FINALLY EVALUATED INTELLIGENCE

PLANNING BY USAMA BIN LADIN TO
HIJACK U.S. AIRPLANE; SUCCESSFUL CIRCUMVENTION OF
SECURITY MEASURES IN U.S. AIRPORT

C05418803

BIN LADIN WAS PLANNING TO EXECUTE
NEW OPERATIONS AGAINST UNITED STATES (U.S.) TARGETS IN THE NEAR
FUTURE. PLANS TO HIJACK A U.S. AIRCRAFT WERE PROCEEDING WELL.   TWO
INDIVIDUALS FROM THE RELEVANT OPERATIONAL TEAM IN THE U.S. HAD
SUCCESSFULLY EVADED SECURITY CHECKS DURING A TRIAL RUN AT "NEW
YORK AIRPORT   BIN LADIN HOPED THAT THE
OPERATION WOULD BE IMPLEMENTED BEFORE THE START OF RAMADAN.

CIRCA 20 DECEMBER.) THE OBJECTIVE OF THE OPERATION IS TO OBTAIN
THE RELEASE OF BLIND SHAYKH 'UMAR AHMAD 'ABD AL-((RAHMAN)), RAMZI
((YOUSEF)) AND MUHAMMAD SADIQ ((ODEH)), A SUSPECT IN THE BOMBING
OF THE U.S. EMBASSY IN NAIROBI, KENYA.
YOUSEF AND RAHMAN WERE CONVICTED OF THE WORLD TRADE CENTER BOMBING
IN NEW YORK. MOHAMMAD SADIQ ODEH
WAS ARRESTED

One could break down the text contained in this document and make several speculations on its meaning. Such speculations carry little value, but the one thing that is crystal clear, is the document shows an implicit knowledge of Bin Laden and his plan, two full years prior to 9/11. The document also shows that this highly specific Intel went all the way to the White House, and therefore, it is at the highest level where the 'breakdown' occurred.

Some suggest it shows a CIA hand in Bin Laden's planning; some suggest the CIA were still tweaking their '9/11 story'. Whatever the case, pleading ignorance and disorganization in regards to 9/11 is simply a form of deception - they knew.

The U.S. Intelligence Community knew of Osama (Usama then) Bin Laden because he was an 'asset' on the CIA's books before 1979; they knew his physical and financial movements. They knew the Mujahideen because they created and armed the Mujahideen to fight the Soviet Union in Afghanistan. They knew Al Qaeda because in the early eighties Al Qaeda was simply a list of contacts that later developed into a network of Islamic mercenaries run by Osama Bin Laden of the CIA to fight the Soviets.

The CIA knew Bin Laden had become dangerous because they had turned on him. They knew he went to Sudan. They knew he went back to Afghanistan. They knew all his movements. They knew his intentions and motives and financial prowess and continued Saudi backing.

Saudi interests still finance Al Qaeda today.

The CIA, NSA, USAFINT, NORAD, and The White House, knew that hijacked airliners used as weapons within the USA was a plausible option for Bin Laden. They saw Bin Laden's men get through airport security in 1998, and did nothing to change security systems. NORAD had run this Hijacked airliner scenario as both paper training exercises, and real exercises - and despite this, after 9/11 Condoleezza Rice and Dick Cheney both said the very idea of an airliner attack was unthinkable, un-planed for, and was never even considered - yet it is clearly outlined in this CIA briefing document, and many more.

Heck, Tom Clancy even used the exact scenario in his bestselling thriller, *Debt of Honor*.

Ignorance can be no excuse for 'not seeing' 9/11 coming. The excuse of ignorance and the Intelligence Community's change of story, suggests at least some level of organized deception in relation to 9/11.

Where the Conspiracy Theorists Fail

The great conspiracy theories surrounding 9/11 boil down to this: the Bush cartel of Rumsfeld, Cheney, Rice, Rove, Powel etc; along with Israel's Mossad, thought up, financed, created, and made 9/11 happen.

This idea is of course, flawed. Most conspiracy theorists have not studied the Cold War history and the Middle Eastern situation well enough.

Firstly, the idea of Al Qaeda hijacking an airliner and crashing it into a target on U.S. soil appears plausible. So let's break it down into its parts:

> 1) As previously stated, U.S. intelligence prior to, and after 9/11, monitors the Middle East terrorist groups through a microscope; secret satellites hover above the region providing super-close-up Infra-red and video images incorporating face recognition

50

software; operatives and assets on the inside have their ears to the ground; the NSA monitors and processes every bit of electronic data, gathered from long range listening devices; they record and scan every phone call with voice recognition software. The CIA knows exactly what is going on because they control the entire situation; although to the untrained eye, the Mideast appears 'out of control'. In our blurred reality there are three splits in thinking here:

a) Radical rogue terror groups, Al Qaeda, and now IS, pose a threat to U.S. interests in the region and are difficult to find and/or eliminate, and;

b) The Mideast situation is always under total U.S. control; not enough military force to shut down and destroy the confidence of the terror cells, but enough (when needed) to contain them, or direct them onto non-compliant regimes, and;

c) The CIA controls the terror groups from within; keeping up a 'lively terror' in order to serve preplanned Middle Eastern outcomes of perpetual civil war and control of OPEC.

2) Prior knowledge of Al Qaeda's 9/11 plan *was* discovered by lower level agencies, proving the low level Intel snooping from even the FBI was good enough to know everything that Al Qaeda was up to, without the super technology of the NSA, NRO, and the CIA, (but there was an attempt to conceal this fact). Once this fact escaped, the Bush group switched to ignorance as its excuse, saying that the Intel wasn't actioned due to dis-organization

between intelligence agencies. 9/11 was, paradoxically, both discovered, and unimaginable at the same time.

The reality is that this kind of intelligence *would not* be scrambled unless by design. It was just too big for that to happen accidentally. For historical comparison read the Pearl Harbor chapter in my previous book, *A Time for Deception.*

3) After the first two aircraft hit the towers, NORAD, America's premier air-defense network, would have been searching their airspace for any other hijacked aircraft, working out their/its course and most likely target, seeing it tracking toward the Pentagon, and scrambling fighters to bring it down.

But Donald Rumsfeld, as it turns out, was in the NORAD control room at the time of the 9/11 hijackings, whilst under his orders, NORAD was conducting a series electronic exercises using real aircraft - a series of exercises of the exact 'multiple airliner hijacking' situation unfolding for real, outside the window.[63]

So once again, why did Rice and Rumsfeld later say the 9/11 scenario was so 'out-there', it was not able to even be imagined?

During the 9/11 attacks, NORAD operators became confused over whether the Al Qaeda hijacked airliners were in the 'real world' or 'exercise'.[64] There were so many 'hijacked airliners' in the air that they would never have been

---

63. Moore: Fahrenheit 9/11
64. Ibid

able to differentiate the real from the electronic.

It was this confusion, created by Donald Rumsfeld, which allowed the third airliner the time needed to hit the Pentagon.

What are the odds?

So to return to the point: yes, Al Qaeda hijacking *one* airliner and using it on U.S. soil may be plausible, (*if you suspend your disbelief of the Intel failure*), but would the third airliner have had the time to reach the Pentagon without 'help'?

It is difficult to prove or disprove the 9/11 false-flag theory short of an admission, and I don't wish to trawl every 9/11 'conspiracy' type evidence here, but it appears highly likely, from the dissemination of the litany of lies propping up the War on Terror, that the following *could* indeed be our reality:

> 1) The Bush cartel did not think 9/11 up, but the NSA, NRO, FBI, and the CIA discovered Al Qaeda's 9/11 plan in every detail.
>
> 2) If they were to allow 9/11 to happen, the military and financial outcomes, and the huge rewards gained would be immense.
>
> A free ticket to wage war anywhere in the Middle East oil ring for decades.
>
> 3) The Bush cartel decided to allow the 9/11 attack to happen; just like FDR decided to 'let' the Japanese attack Pearl Harbor.

2403 Americans died at Pearl Harbor; a noble lie for the greater good - the greater good of the Military Industrial Complex, the Federal Reserve, and big oil. (If you disagree with, or can't believe the Pearl Harbor false flag theory, please read the Pearl Harbor chapter in my previous book, *A Time for Deception*).

Was 9/11 for the greater good?

If so, the greater good is not yours or mine.

I accept many will not buy this 9/11 theory; some will think the Bush cartel orchestrated the entire thing; some will believe in their ignorance and innocence.

But as Sir Arthur Conan Doyle's Sherlock Holmes famously said: "When you have eliminated all other avenues, whatever remains, however improbable, must be the truth."

The reality here is hard to know for certain, but what is certain, is that believing the propaganda, and buying the deception, blurs the reality we so desperately seek. The prevailing illusion, created by expert deception planners, offers us an easy out.

4

The Rosin Affidavit

The Rosin Affidavit is important to this subject matter because it opens up and exposes the post WWII Military/Industrial deception from the inside; and we can literately see the deception unfold across the decades.

Dr. Rosin

[D]r. Carol Rosin was the first woman corporate manager of Fairchild Industries and was spokesperson for Werner Von Braun in the last [4] years of his life. She founded the Institute for Security and Co-operation in Outer Space in Washington D.C. and has testified before Congress on many occasions about space based weapons. Von Braun revealed to Dr. Rosin a plan to justify weapons in space, based on hoaxing an extraterrestrial threat.[65]

Von Braun was the Nazi rocket engineer behind the V2 terror rocket attacks on London during WWII. Under Operation Paperclip, he was transferred stateside to continue his work, eventually heading the newly formed Marshall Space Flight Center. Von Braun was also the chief architect of the Saturn V launch vehicle. He died in 1977, aged 65.

---

65. *The Disclosure Project' website. Dr. S.M. Greer (MD)*

Dr. Carol Rosin closely assisted Von Braun from 1973 until his death in 1977.[66]

History's Testimony: A Familiar Pattern

In her infamous affidavit, given on May 9, 2001 - a full four months before the 9/11 attacks - Dr. Rosin testified to the gathered press at a Disclosure Project press conference, that between 1974 and 1977, Werner Von Braun had disclosed to her the true nature of the global deception. She said:

> [T]he strategy that was being used to educate the public and decision makers was to use scare tactics . . . That was how we identified an enemy. . . first Russians were going to be considered the enemy.

> Then terrorists would be identified.

> Then we were going to identify third-world country crazies . . .

> The next enemy was asteroids. Now at this point he [Von Braun] kind of chuckled the first time he said it. Asteroids - against asteroids we are going to build space-based weapons.

> And the funniest one of all was what he called aliens - extraterrestrials. That would be the final scare. And over and over during the four years that I knew him and was giving speeches for him, he would bring up that last card. "And remember Carol, the last card is the alien card. We

> are going to have to build space-based weapons against aliens, and all of it is a lie."[67]

---

66. *The Affidavit of Dr. Carol Rosin to the Disclosure Project, May 9, 2001*
67. *Ibid*

Rosin also stated that she had told her husband in the year of 1977, that the 1991 Invasion of Iraq, and the first Gulf War had already been planned.

She learned this at a meeting held in the Fairchild Industries 'war-room'.

"The tone in the meeting was that the (1991) War in Iraq would go ahead regardless; and was necessary in the greater scheme of deception planning."[68]

Of course, the main points for us, in regards to Mideast terror and today's notion of the declared war against the abstract notion of terror, are clear:

> 1) *"The strategy that was being used to educate the public and decision makers was to use scare tactics."*

As WWII's end morphed into the Cold War against the Soviet Union, fear was going to be used against the public, as per Nazi population control doctrine. Note also that Rosin suggests that 'decision makers' would also be manipulated along with the public. The Nazi mantra was: Fear equals control. According to the Rosin affidavit, U.S. deception strategists, desiring full public compliance for some preplanned reason, would also incite a deep, encapsulating public fear, vis-à-vis the Nazi propaganda machine.

> 2) *"First Russians were going to be considered the enemy."*

And boy did we fear the USSR and nuclear annihilation. The Soviet fear campaign was media driven, with continued and repeated images of

---

68. *The Affidavit of Dr. Carol Rosin to the Disclosure Project, May 9, 2001*

mushroom clouds, kids forced to 'duck-and-cover' in schools, and our nuclear annihilation at the hands of blood thirsty Soviet psychopaths.

Check. The first enemy to fear was the Russians.

3) *"Then terrorists would be identified."*

As per Rosin's check sheet, from 1978, the CIA armed and midwifed the Islamic Fundamentalist movement into existence. In a nice twist, Brzezinski used the new 'terrorists' to remove the old USSR. However a combination of terrible treatment in all regional sects, arming, and funding in the tens of billions through corrupt conduit banks, leading the Afghans into a bloody holy-war for personal gain, and then promptly turning their backs on them, leaving them to fester into a seething morass of anti Western hate, the CIA fulfilled their objective. Harry Truman regretfully said: "I never would have agreed to the formulation of the Central Intelligence Agency back in forty-seven, if I had known it would become the American Gestapo."[69]

4) *"Then we were going to identify third-world country crazies."*

Throughout the 70's, 80's, & 90,s - to the present day, the CIA has picked, groomed, and installed a string of dictators in third-world Mideast countries. When required, the U.S. military deposed them in a series of lucrative wars. Colonel Gaddafi and Saddam Hussein are the most well known.

---

69. *Harry. S. Truman on CIA Covert Operations - National Archives (Declassified NND-947003)*

Third-world dictators fit hand in glove with Islamic Fundamentalist terrorism because they usually hate each other. Third world country crazies also fits with the ideals and rise of ISIS.

5) The rest of Rosin's/Von Braun's 'enemy' scenarios are to come, (Asteroids & Alien invasion) but for our needs in clearing a blurred Mideast reality, Rosins sequentially correct chain of deception, leaked to her by Von Braun in 1973, tolls a very familiar bell.

5

The Axis of Evil

President George W. Bush first barked the phrase 'Axis of Evil' during his January, 2002 State of the Union Address.[70]

Like any propaganda campaign, the phrase was, from that point on, repeated and repeated and repeated, so as we would never forget who the new 'enemy' was.

The Axis was Iran, Iraq, and North Korea.[71]

The term 'Axis' was clearly used to make us link the Nazis, Italy, and Japan – the axis forces of WWII – to reinforce the 'evilness' of the new enemy.[72]

Iran and Iraq are clearly the two Mideast nations that the Bush cartel wanted to target; but because an evil axis has three evil nations, North Korea was thrown in the mix, containing, of course, a crazed third-world dictator, albeit of his own making, a nuclear weapons and power generation dream, and very importantly *not* being an OPEC country.

We were told these axis nations were ruled by evil governments that funded and harbored terrorists, weapons of mass destruction, poison gas, and secret nuclear weapons programs.

In our minds, the Axis of Evil tied together these common enemies, rallying the country in support of the 'War on Terror'.

70. *The U.S. National 2002 State of the Union Address*
71. *Ibid*
72. *Chomsky Interview: Our Own Private Bin Laden*

Welcome to psyops; the psychological manipulation of the Western public.

We were/are all convinced that these countries were/are evil, and pose a clear threat to our lives.

Post 9/11, it is very easy to make people not just scared, but terrified. A terror inconsistent with the risk.

Of course, later proof showed that absolutely all of 'crimes' of which the evil axis were accused, were false.

But they could have been real!

They could still be! Couldn't they?

Such is the incredible effectiveness of the War on Terror's psyops deception campaign that we will probably never be able to think otherwise. It is so effective though, because an element of truth exists. Exaggeration is the word.

Let's break it down:

1) Iran: CIA medaling in Iran, solely for oil company profit, such as deposing the popular Shah and installing a puppet, triggered anti U.S. mindsets within Iran during the 1980's.

2) With the rise of Islamic Fundamentalism, Iran will contain terrorists. The U.S. however, (whether sticking to Von Braun's leaked plan or not) has created this sentiment so well, it may never change.

3) It stands to reason then, that some Iranians pose a threat to us; but a very small one. Iran itself would not possibly want a conventional war with the U.S. It would be counter-productive, and certainly un-winnable when our non-conventional weapons capabilities are considered (and Putin's staff would've brought the new Iranian President, Hassan Rouhani,

quickly up to speed. Rouhani took over from
Mahmoud Ahmadinejad, (often referred to as
armored-dinner-jacket), who served eight years as
Iran's president, from 2005 to 2013.
Iran is not a country friendly to the U.S. Although, if
they 'did-as-to-us', as we 'did-as-to-them', would we
be friendly?

Despite this Iran complies with, and enforces OPEC
agreements, serving U.S. oil interests.

For U.S. citizens, a level of threat exists from within
Iran, but is low.

[Y]ou are 1904% more likely to die in an auto wreck than
from terrorist action from any nation.[73]

There was no link between Iran and Al Qaeda, like there was
no link between Al Qaeda and Saddam's regime. Al Qaeda's
goal is to depose U.S. puppet dictators.

Iran supports Palestinians however, which brings us
back to the Israel/Palestinian paradox. The U.S. (certainly at
that time) could not have people supporting Palestinians.

Iran had no nuclear weapons program; but did seek
nuclear power generation. The spent fuel from nuclear
power generation however, could be later weaponized.
Although I suggest that if Iran wanted weapons grade
plutonium 239, they would have created a secret processing
facility, but did not.

It is more likely that Iran needed to be pulled into
line, and bow down to the emerging nuclear power
authority, but that is another story.

---

73. Engelhardt: *The American Empire Project*

Iran is listed as an enemy, and is called an enemy of the free world; Iran however, is an oil corporate ally in many respects. Iranian soldiers will also be used by the U.S. to contain IS militants to the correct areas: Iraq and Syria.

A Stitch in Time: The Iraq Pattern

In 1964 Vietnam was invaded by United States forces in what would become ten year occupation. Vietnam's invasion was pre-planned. The key points are:

> 1) A triggering act of aggression from the 'enemy' was needed to justify the invasion – the weak, or fake, Gulf of Tonkin attack was LBJ's trigger.

> 2) The public, through a comprehensive fear campaign, was convinced the invasion was necessary – to stop the spread of communism. We now realize that this was garbage. The goal to generate massive, revenge based patriotism.

> 3) Massive amounts of small arms were *given* to Vietnam by the U.S. The country was flooded with arms. Puppet governments were installed in the South, and a charismatic 'terrorist' leader united the enemy in the North.

> 4) The war was an oil war: Vietnam's undersea oilfields were pinpointed and mapped.

> 5) The war was pre-emptive – Vietnam had never attacked the U.S., and had zero ability, or desire, to attack the United States at home.

6) The unprovoked invasion was justified on the grounds of 'self defense', making it a 'just war'.

Fear campaign. Triggering event. Call for Patriotism. Pre-emptive invasion for self defense. Deception to justify Occupation.[74]

Iraq's 2003 invasion was pre-planned, and followed a similar pattern:

1) 9/11 was the trigger, whether a false-flag or not.

2) Fear of a terrorist attack was generated through intensive media hype. What would 9/11 have been without television? I don't say this to be callous – it is just a pure fact that 9/11's intense TV coverage spread fear like plague – playing right into the terrorists hands. What would terrorism be if we did not televise it?

3) Via the CIA, arms have been flooded into the Mideast since 1978.

4) Iraq was an oil war: controlling the region and limiting its outputs is key to the oil price.

5) The war was pre-emptive: Iraq did not attack or assist in an attack on U.S. soil, nor did they have the means to do so.

6) Iraq's invasion was justified on the grounds of self defense, making it a just war.

Technical differences between invasion Vietnam and

---

74. Stone. *A Time for Deception*

invasion Iraq exist, but the basic blueprint is the same.

> [T]he report, the 15th released by the 911 commission staff, concluded, "We have no credible evidence that Iraq and al-Qaida cooperated on attacks against the United States."[75]

> [I]n making the case for war in Iraq, Bush administration officials frequently cited what they said were Saddam's decade-long contacts with al-Qaida operatives. They stopped short of claiming that Iraq was directly involved in the Sept. 11 attacks, but critics say Bush officials left that impression with the American public.[76]

Most coalition soldiers in Iraq believed their mission was to 'avenge' Saddam's role in 9/11.

Archangels: The Arc of Instability

On the paradox of the 'Arc of Instability', it is best to cite Tom Engelhardt:

> [I]n a February 2006 address to the American Legion focused on his Global War on Terror, for instance, President Bush typically said: "Slowly but surely, we're helping to transform the broader Middle East from an arc of instability in to an arc of freedom. And as freedom reaches more people in this vital region, we'll have new allies in the war on terror, and new partners in the cause of moderation in the Muslim world, and in the cause of peace."[77]

---

75. *NBC News msnbc.com staff and news service reports updated 6/16/2004*
76. *Ibid*
77. *Engelhardt. Who Won Iraq, June 2014*

Bush's arc swept from Libya in North Africa, and up through Syria and Iraq in the Middle East.

13 years after the launch of the War on Terror, and significant U.S. military focus in each of these three countries, we can clearly see the U.S./CIA's stabilizing effect.

The archangels - the bringers of peace - have manipulated and divided theses countries, sending them spiraling into a living hell of perpetual civil war.

Part Three

The Rise of IS

6

Out of the Blue

In this particular book I wanted to avoid the sink-hole of the 9/11 debate.

Most have their opinions, and proving otherwise essentially draws in a morass of compelling, but circumstantial evidence.

Nevertheless, 9/11 is impossible to avoid, because 9/11 is the one and only justification for the Invasion of Iraq; and the invasion of Iraq is the single biggest cause of the rise of ISIS.

Using 9/11 to justify Invasion Iraq (not linked to Al Qaeda, and less linked to them than Saudi Arabia) shows deception planning on the United States' behalf; and deception planning always underlies illegal activity – as it certainly has in historical deception operations against the taxpaying public.

During war deception fools ones enemy; during peace deception covers actions that would fail to gain public support.

The fact that the CIA knew of the continued Saudi financing behind Al Qaeda, and the fact that this has never been considered worthy of mention, let alone investigation -

the invasions of Afghanistan and Iraq being more important - is not just odd, it's confirmation that the CIA *wants* Al Qaeda to exist.

Senator Bob Graham is quoted on the record:

> "I think there is very compelling evidence that at least some of the terrorists were assisted not just in financing — although that was part of it — by a sovereign foreign government and that we have been derelict in our duty to track that down, make the further case, or find the evidence that would indicate that that is not true and we can look for other reasons why the terrorists were able to function so effectively in the United States."

IS, the new terrorist enemy, is nothing more than outgrowth of Al Qaeda, brainwashed by twisting religion into human atrocity.

The militants believe in their manufactured cause; and likewise, the Allied coalition soldiers believe in their manufactured cause - while those that pull the strings, the puppet masters of this sick pantomime, sit in their ivory towers counting their profit.

By loosely tying 9/11 to Saddam's Iraq, its shows a preparedness use lies to achieve corporate objectives.

If 9/11 did happen as per the Bush explanation – genuine, unavoidable terrorist action that defeated the NSA, CIA, FBI, The White House, and the NORAD air defense network, despite multiple, specific, and detailed warnings that it was coming as described – then a 'mop up' of Al Qaeda camps in Afghanistan would be considered a 'normal' military response. Al Qaeda was in Afghanistan because that's where they formed. They were also in Pakistan.

Despite these anti-terror operations, and the killing of Osama Bin Laden, Islamic terror Jihad has exploded.

How do we explain that?

One answer is: this is the way the CIA wants it. If so, they want it this way because non-compliant dictators and their armies can be knocked out by 'rogue Islamic rebel groups', giving the U.S. a buffer of plausible deniability. For example the non-compliant Libyan dictator, Muammar Gaddafi, assassinated October 20, 2011 by CIA engineered rebels. Libya has spiraled into a leaderless wild-west, and a hot-bed in which more terrorist groups will thrive.

Feeling scared?

Can Libya be fixed?

Seems unlikely. Libya resembles America's wild-west, gangs of New York style, corrupt, ruthless, and leaderless - except chock-full of pickup trucks and machine guns. They can't have the shoulder fired stinger or Igla infra-red anti aircraft rockets though; they might shoot down the CIA drones that monitor them and 'keep then in the zoo'.

But the most recent and shocking oddity, and the most compelling reason behind my writing this book, is this: despite being a 70 billion dollar a year intelligence goliath, according to the CIA, the rise of IS in Syria and Iraq - came 'out of the blue'.

Blurred Intelligence

After the bizarre litany of 9/11 intelligent 'failures', the Intelligence Community has consistently failed to improve.

In fact they haven't improved since 1940.

Their excuse - despite massive and accurate intelligence being collected and available in time - the excuse for the failure to stop or avoid the December 7, 1941 Japanese attack at Pearl Harbor was blamed on ineptitude.

Missing 9/11 was blamed on ineptitude.

They *new* all of Al Qaeda's movements and plans in time, so just like Pearl Harbor, Intel collection was successful, they just 'messed up' - again.

And blow me down, if it hasn't happened again.

Despite occupying Iraq for the best part of a decade. Despite growing, developing, and possessing history's most advanced global 'big brother' surveillance systems; and despite sucking in an annual mega-budget of over $68 billion per year, the CIA claims to have completely missed the build up, recruitment, and rise of IS.

> [I]t's quite an achievement, especially when you consider its (the U.S. intelligence community's) one downside: it has a terrible record of getting anything right in a timely way. Never have so many had access to so much information about our world and yet been so unprepared for whatever happens in it.[78] (brackets added)

With the mathematical odds stacked against the likelihood of such failures, one has to ask: are these Intelligence failures by accident or by design?

The Chaos Paradox

The first strange tactical moves in Iraq after control was seized by the U.S. occupying forces, was to dismantle Iraq's 350,000 man army, reducing its numbers to around 12,000;

---

78. *Engelhardt. Failure is Success: How American Intelligence Works in the Twenty-First Century. September 2014*

and to remove Iraq's airforce.[79]

IS militants, although they look tough on TV, could not have forced a state of civil war in Iraq and Syria with only a few thousand militants if Iraq's military was, or had been, maintained in full.

Was the U.S. invasion force unwittingly creating the conditions needed for IS to thrive?

Or did they do so purposefully?

Was another regression to the stone-age needed to keep the foot of control firmly on Mideast's throat?

An orchestrated and continual civil war in the Mideast countries regresses them, keeps them in technology debt, and crushes their ability to organize and control their own destinies.

Right now, IS is that civil war.

IS exists because the CIA allows it to exist. ISIS is a corralled and controlled CIA tool, whose purpose is to create civil war, keep the region educatively and technologically in debt, and spread a deep fear of terrorism via social media.

A more extreme, but unproven premise, is that of Chechnya's President, that the CIA has plants within ISIL, suggesting IS is purely a CIA creation. This level of clarity however, is not currently possible to know, but several indicators raise eyebrows:

> 1) The CIA, FBI, and U.S. government allowing Saudi Interests to *continue* to fund Al Qaeda - Al Qaeda is linked to IS. And;

---

79. Engelhardt. *Who Won Iraq*, June 2014

2) Suggesting that Al Qaeda has distanced itself from IS, as if these Siamese twins are unrelated.

3) The immediate reduction of Iraq's armies post 2003, making Iraq vulnerable to IS and totally reliant on U.S. assistance - giving the U.S. total control of IS's spread.

> nb: the disbanding of Iraq's army put 338,000 men on the breadline; few Shia Muslims will side with IS, but some may, further fueling IS's rise.

4) Ensuring the USAF is the only air force in the region gives total, unopposed dominance. This dominance is only used to corral and contain, prolonging the 'conflict'. The prolonged conflict supplies U.S. justification for further 'assistance' or occupation.

5) The ridiculous 'intelligence failures' shows deception in play. This deception, when viewed critically, shows *support* for Islamic terrorists.

6) The fact that IS is still there re-enforces this fact.

7) The suggestion that ISIS came 'out of the blue' is clearly garbage, in a region occupied by U.S. forces since 2003; which the CIA monitors via satellite, undercover agents, and a raft of other top-secret Intel gathering techniques.

Some believe that Iraq and Syria have turned to custard for the United States; saying nothing has worked out as planned.

I suggest the opposite. It's working perfectly.

When IS has done the CIA's job, they will quickly be brought under control – or will be wiped out altogether.

Some cite the destruction of Iraq's oil infrastructure as proof of U.S. failure - and I drop to the ground laughing. In Iraq's last rebuild, U.S. companies, including Halliburton, were given massive contracts; their first task – rebuild Iraq's oil infrastructure.[80]

The cost doesn't bother U.S. oil companies one bit, because the rebuild money comes from the U.S. tax-take in a maelstrom money siphon. Paul Bremer (leader of the occupational authority of Iraq after the 2003 invasion) also said: "Iraq can cover its rebuild costs with future oil revenue".[81]

The Invasion and occupation of Iraq alone has exceeded two-trillion dollars.[82]

That's why the CEOs and major shareholders in the companies of the Military Industrial Alliance can't get the smiles off of their faces.

A Blurred Reality

So have we cleared our blurred reality?

Of course not; the CIA's deception planning and propaganda machine masks the secret and illegal facts well. It should; it has taken decades to perfect. Where it doesn't or can't mask the incriminating facts, it makes the lies so big that it becomes impossible for us to believe anything else.

What is clear though, is this:

1) Although motivated by the 1947 Israeli takeover of

---

80. *Our Own Private Bin Laden*
81. *Ibid*
82. *Engelhardt. Who Won Iraq, June 2014*

Palestine, IS, its backers and motives, are in a completely separate realm to that of Palestinians. The IS mindset stems from a combination of Islamic brainwashing, and resistance to U.S. medaling in the Mideast since 1979.

2) Within the Middle East, the U.S. functions as an Empire.

3) The CIA functions as the Middle East's Gestapo.

4) They do so, not just to keep terrorists from our boarders, but to control the flow, availability, and therefore the price of Mideast oil.

4) These Mideast terrorist groups are armed, and to some extent controlled, by the CIA and Saudi Arabian financers. This is clear - it is the extent of this 'assistance' that remains blurred.

5) These terror cells are real; their members believe in Jihad; they hate America.

6) The first terror cells were a creation of the CIA's arming and nursing of the Mujahideen. Today they (IS) are 'allowed' to exist so as to:

a) Heighten our fear of terror attacks, or a second 911 on U.S. soil, justifying Iraq's occupation under the guise of self defense, and;

b) To topple non-compliant dictators inside the Mideast oil ring, maintaining a buffer of plausible deniability for illegal, ruthless control of the old British oil Empire - this charade is transparent to many, including Vladimir Putin, and many American politicians.

c) To trigger destructive Middle Eastern civil wars; because the Mideast cannot be allowed to become technologically advanced or educated as this would threaten U.S. control. A continued and periodic 'regression' via CIA triggered civil wars ensures U.S./corporate control over the Mideast going forward.

d) This is of course denied, and the prevailing illusion of terror (although very real) is exacerbated and exaggerated; the purpose of the prevailing illusion is to make us feel good about our 'just war'.

6) 9/11, whether orchestrated entirely by the Bush cartel; allowed to happen; or whether it happened because of incompetence, has achieved the patriotism and public support needed to occupy and pulverize Iraq for the purposes of the above reasons.

7) The $68 billion per year Intelligence Community uses ignorance and incompetence as its excuse for 'not seeing [insert terrorist act] coming' - for what other excuse is there?

8) The façade of deception is crumbling. The charade is transparent.

The solution to this mess is not the purpose of this work; the tragic mess, purposefully created by a corporate controlled U.S. government and its CIA Gestapo, has gone on for so long now that any solution will not be simple.

The first and most critical element however, is obvious: to reduce society's dependence on oil and petroleum, so as the world can emerge from its corporate enforced technology dark-age.

In the domestic market, oil should by now, be obsolete technology. Electric cars, solar energy, Tesla's hidden and classified technology for the wireless transduction and beaming from the magnetosphere and the electro-jet, would clean the environment, halt global warming, free the Middle East of tyranny, and over time, stop the Islamic Terrorist mindset - a pure creation of the oil industry.

But what effect would a global need for less oil have on the petroleum exporting countries?

To this point, former Saudi Arabian Oil Minister, Sheikh Yamani said: "The stone age didn't end because we ran out of stones."[83]

The end of the oil-age will send the Mideast back to the stone-age - but would they be any worse off than they are now?

Some need for oil products will always remain, so not all oil production will cease - but as much as 50% is clearly possible.

When we can finally leave the Middle East alone, eventually, they will leave us alone.

But of course we can't leave them alone - not until we remove the need to control the OPEC country's oil quotas.

---

83. Friedman. *Hot, Flat, & Crowded: Why the World needs a Green Revolution*

Final Thoughts

The one thing clouding our perception - at all levels - is our trust in the CIA, and our own personal level of acceptance of political deception – deception that intentionally creates a blurred reality.

The End

References:

1. *Stone. A Time for Deception*
2. *Ibid*
3. *McBeth. British Oil Policy*
4. *Ibid*
5. *Marshall Douglas Smith. Black Gold Hot Gold*
6. *Spingola. The Power Elite Playbook*
7. *Ibid*
8. *Noam Chomsky. Power & Terror in Our Times*
9. *Moshe. A History of Palestine, pgs634–1099. Cambridge University Press.*
10. *Ibid*
11. *Ibid*
12. *Ibid*
13. *wikipedia. David Ben Gurion*
14. *Biblical scripture relating to Zionism, not of course, WWII*
15. *Taken from, Noam Chomsky. Fateful Triangle: The United States, Israel, and the Palestinians*
16. *Taken from, Cragg (1997) pgs 57 & 116.*
17. *Morris. The Birth of the Palestinian Refugee Problem Revisited*
18. *Ibid*
19. *Chomsky. Power & Terror in Our Times*
20. *The American Empire Project*
21. *OPEC, wikipedia*
22. *wikipedia: Hamas*
23. *BBC News, 26/1/2006, Who are Hamas?*
24. *Hamas Covenant, 1988 version*
25. *Pew Research Centre: Mapping the Global Muslim Population*
26. *Ibid*
27. *The official CIA Fact-book, and; Mackenzie. The Origin of Kurdish: Transactions of Philological Society, pgs 68–86*
28. *Van Buren. Seven Worst Case Scenarios in the Battle with the Islamic State (10.16.2014)*
29. *Marshal Douglas Smith. Black Gold Hot Gold*
30. *Farrell. Reich of the Black Sun*
31. *Ibid*
32. *Ibid*
33. *Lyne. Pentagon Aliens*

References

34. Spingola. *The Power Elite Playbook*
35. Chomsky. *Fateful Triangle: The United States, Israel, and the Palestinians*
36. Farrell. *Reich of the Black Son*
37. *Ibid*
38. Laos, Cambodia, and Vietnam; the French loosing Indochina as a colony in 1954 after military defeat by Ho Chi Minh's, Viet Minh at Diem Bin Phu
39. There were two alleged NVN attacks; August 2nd & 4th. An FOIA NSA document stated the attack on the 4th did not happen.
40. FOIA: *Operation Northwoods Briefing Document (Facsimile)*
41. Stone. *A Time for Deception*, pg81
42. Stone. *The Cover of War research; interview with Hòng Nguyen*
43. Spingola. *The Power Elite Playbook*
44. United Nations Security Council Records
45. Stone. *A Time for Deception*, pg91
46. Marshall Douglas Smith. *Black Gold Hot Gold*
47. *Ibid*
48. Documentary: *Our Own Private Bin Laden*
49. *Ibid*
50. *Ibid*
51. *Ibid*
52. *Ibid*
53. *Ibid*
54. Zbigniew Brzezinski. *Le Nouvel Observeteur*, 1998
55. *Ibid*
56. Documentary: *Our Own Private Bin Laden*
57. Chomsky. *Power and Terror in Our Times*
58. *Ibid*
59. Documentary: *Oil Factor*
60. Documentary: *Our Own Private Bin Laden*
61. The History Channel. *Conspiracy Files*
62. FOIA: National Security Archive. View online at: http://www2.gwu.edu/~nsarchiv/NSAEBB/NSAEBB381/
63. Moore: *Fahrenheit 9/11*
64. *Ibid*
65. The Disclosure Project' website. Dr. S.M. Greer (MD)
66. The Affidavit of Dr. Carol Rosin to the Disclosure Project, May 9, 2001
67. *Ibid*
68. *Ibid*

References

69. Harry. S. Truman on CIA Covert Operations - National Archives (Declassified NND-947003)
70. The U.S. National 2002 State of the Union Address
71. Ibid
72. Chomsky Interview: Our Own Private Bin Laden
73. Engelhardt: The American Empire Project
74. Stone. A Time for Deception
75. NBC News msnbc.com staff and news service reports updated 6/16/2004 6:48:59 PM ET
76. Ibid
77. Engelhardt. Who Won Iraq, June 2014
78. Engelhardt. Failure is Success: How American Intelligence Works in the Twenty-First Century. September 2014
79. Engelhardt. Who Won Iraq, June 2014
80. Our Own Private Bin Laden
81. Ibid
82. Engelhardt. Who Won Iraq, June 2014
83. Friedman. Hot, Flat, & Crowded: Why the World needs a Green Revolution